MINDFUL

Poems

of

Hope

and

Experience

Martin Stepek

To Jill
With best
...

ISBN: 978-0-9930514-3-2

Published by
Fleming Publications
Fleming House
Glasgow

qᆍP

Introduction

I am writing this while sitting in a park in Warsaw, before I head to a business meeting. It's a beautiful warm sunny day. A large fountain makes a lovely soft tune for me, and the sunshine on the flying water really does make it seem like diamonds or ice are being poured up and down in vast quantities. Two elderly Polish ladies are sitting on the bench beside me, chatting gently in that pleasant tongue that my father and his sister spoke when they didn't want me to know what they were talking about.

It seems an idyllic place to write, an easy place to feel happiness and hope. Yet this is the place those two old ladies probably saw completely in ruins in their childhood. The city almost completely uninhabited and with ninety percent of its building deliberately blown up by the retreating Nazi forces. The two ladies then lived through Stalin's brutal revenge on Poland's culture and way of life. Only in 1990 did the two ladies witness a truly independent Poland come back into being. By that time the Polish people had rebuilt brick by brick, statue by statue, Poland's historic centre, and now in 2015 it flourishes as a major European city, albeit with all the social, economic and environmental challenges our species has created.

In the attempt to create we must be mindful, and for that reason I would encourage everyone to practise creative arts of any kind,

Mindfulness could be described as healthy attainment of the poetic or artistic sensibility. That heightened awareness so captured in certain classic lines:

Ae fond kiss and then we sever (RobertBurns)
A world in a grain of sand (William Blake)
The force that through the green fuse drives the flower (Dylan Thomas)

Mindfulness allows us - trains us - to notice fully all that is going on in the present moment. This includes our five senses: smell, taste, touch, hearing, sight. It also includes our mental states and what the mind produces, but it asks us to postpone and sometimes let go of our reactions to momentary events. This is because frequently our minds create responses so out of proportion and so skewed that it means we miss the fullness of these moments.

Imagine Robert Burns, Blake or Thomas were too pre-occupied with their everyday life problems - and all three had more than their fair share - to fully notice things. The fond kiss would just fade from memory. The grain of sand would have been lost in the millions of other grains. And the life force that Dylan Thomas noticed would have been missed completely had he been thinking about his poverty at the time.

I've subtitled this short volume *Of Hope and Experience.* I have found mindfulness to be a beacon of hope in a life that has had its challenges and in a world where sometimes the news makes everything appear bleak. These poems are based on and arise from experience. We can only ever have experiences in the present moment, therefore to develop experience we need to be there in the moment. Most people, most of the time, aren't fully present. Rather their minds wander to past events, alternatives to reality such as fantasising or daydreaming, or are focussed on plans or concerns for the future. This is how we have evolved to think. In doing so it has obviously helped us survive as a species; our very presence is the evidence for that. But at what cost to us? What is the point of existing if we miss out on most of what we experience while alive

For There is Hope was published after people emailed me to say that my poetry had helped them come to terms with their own losses, whether related to Poland, the war, or other unrelated matters. In short it was the healing power of deep empathy at work. So too with this book, *Mindful Poems.* Of course, as with all publications, I hope you enjoy it - or parts of it. But more than this, I hope you find in some of the poems or even in a single line or phrase, something that sparks a realisation about the inordinate beauty and awe of being alive. Or that it brings you hope and a smile when you feel down or confused, lonely or cynical. And I hope it inspires some of you to take up writing or some other art for your own happiness and mental wellbeing.

You put something out there
maybe nothing happens
but sometimes
days, weeks, even years later
you get an email
it says, "I'm crying as I write this."

Something I put out there
tore through all the barriers
the massively thick walls
of defensiveness and denial
and broke the heart
and in the breaking
began the process of healing
we call tears

Words put out there

when morning wakes the distant sun
and echoes speak of times gone past
day breaks, cascades its beauty
onto the earth like an ocean spray
the reflection of a blackbird
flying just above the horizon
skims across a large puddle
in a field full of jackdaws
and the world smells of joy

***

after the dawn [1]
before there was wondering
there were wonders
the black of the night
the soft light of the moon
the taste of sleep and dreams

[1] Based on 'Before' by John Guzlowski

so much distraction in life
the vibrant range of music
dramatic images on TV
yet three times today
I walked
just walked
to feel alive
to touch base

***

everyone looking
for what's missing
desperately searching

if we stop searching
we won't curl up and die
in the moments of not searching
we are free

a destructive thought appears
I let it go with accepting grace
to let it stay would mean death
to a million moments
poisoned by pointlessness

***

god is a state of mind
a state of your mind
a state of my mind
it doesn't need the word
god to exist
god just is
it sits within us
without religion
or ritual or prayer
it feels a lot like peace
but you don't need
to believe in god
to know god

I play in the field of life
exploring every inch
loving the rain
as it soaks my hair
stopping every now and then
to turn an insect
trapped on its back

I play till night
when I am tired
I go to bed
and put out the light

***

it was a long time ago
many dreams and hopes
have sailed by since
it's easy to live in the mirage past
or the imagined future
but there's only one place to be
and only one moment to experience
the miracle of being aware
of being alive

laugh in the sunlight and rain
the slightest sound of rustled leaves
I think only of my love for you
that can never die down

this spirit contains, it seems
a space where there grows
and blows a joy that comes
from beginning to understand

smiling in sun and breeze
it shakes free everywhere
I am in control of my thoughts
like wind caught in my hands

(after Fernando Pessoa)

only the moment matters
in the moment we can breathe
see all of life around us
this is our fulfilment
our eternity
the magnificence of raw existence

***

it's quiet and peaceful
a piano plays in the distance
daylight still at nine
a fine May day
the wind blows the trees
on a grassy knoll

***

caresses fell on him
like a cloud descends
a mountain peak
till nothing was visible
but the colour of her passion
and the rainbow streaks
of her embrace

brilliance, already here
in the pub with friends
quiet laughter
catching up with small talk news
later, silent darkness
the still beauty of night
and the prospect of the new dawn
rebirth, hope
what else can a sentient being want?

***

teetotal beer
eases my mind
alcohol free
totally sober
I quench my thirst
soak in pure awareness
0.5% volume
ice cold
straight from the fridge
at peace with non-alcohol culture
hangover-free in the morning
a Scot without alcohol

there's snow on the banking
darkness is falling
the trees seem to shiver

***

unwind the load

***

one verse of the Tao te Ching
lifts you higher
than if you read
the entire canon
of western philosophy

***

I run with a sledge downhill
with my two kids on board
seems centuries ago
they were so young
slopes, freedom
and the chance to run
the wind makes a cape
for my shoulders

whatever befalls
is the gift you were granted
take it and give thanks
for seeing the glory of the day

***

I go
go with the flow
the flow of pain and no pain
the flow of words and no words
the flow of grief and joy
and the joy to know grief
the words to express no words
the purity even of pain
the flow

***

the day starts
it has no purpose
no direction
but it's beautiful
and serves the startling mass
of life forms

the rose does not try to be beautiful
does not moan when its death is near
does not regret a moment of its life

***

the universe is colourful and joyful
clothed in rain and snow
shining like a lantern in the night
dancing in the heavens
waking the dead
with the song of rebirth
moment by precious moment

***

I recognise
but forget
that I should trust
the flow of things
that emerge in their own time
within their own structure
unshaped, unready

I turned on the radio
Roberta Flack sang
The First Time Ever I Saw Your Face
such beauty through the speakers
'like the trembling heart of a captive bird'
it was all I could do not to stop time
and abide in her purity for all eternity

***

vast skies in the Australian desert
waves that don't move
we slide surf glide like condors
the forest is Bohemian
but best of all is self-order
and forgiveness

***

in the startling morning
let's dance the dawn
sing the song-birds' tune

the train sets off
I sit still
as we enter a dark tunnel

the dark tunnel
in my mind

the dark tunnel
is my mind

we pass through it
back into the light

***

in simplicity strength
in quietness power
in solitude peace

***

Autumn declares that growing old
is inherently beautiful

the miracle is not to walk on water
said Thich Nhat Hanh
the miracle, he said
is to walk on the Earth
the miracle
is to be aware you are alive
appreciate your life

***

the sun at close of day
streaks its rays so low
the shadows
stretch on to the golden sea
and starlings with purple and yellow
gem-like feathers
dance in the blue-darkened sky
as I wait for you
the sun sets behind the distant
highland hills
Hamilton settles in the night
a last black-green silhouette
of a slim silver birch
bows to one last streak of sunlight

What a time we have
from dawn to dusk
Spring to Winter
birth to death
I'll sit with you awhile
and hold your hand
while we still have time

***

The birds around the hunting lodge
perform an unbridled symphony
to celebrate momentary sunshine

***

luscious lilac flowers defiantly grow
through the barbed wire fence
by the old stone bridge
over the railway line

I thought I'd like the high speed rail
now I know
I prefer the old slow route
more stations, more stops
but that's my way

***

Autumn sunlight at Chatelherault
the trees show off
their twilight glory
in reds, yellows and golds

***

I watch the day go by
nothing is urgent
so I do nothing
but clear my mind
and watch the day

***

there is something to be said
for saying nothing
from time to time

every action has its effects
so for a simple life
reduce actions
say less
do less
create fewer ripples
and consider carefully
what actions to take

***

on my lap
*The Sutra of the Eight Realisations
of the Great Beings*
the passing breeze teaches me
joy and impermanence

***

don't disturb the silence
it tells secrets
we don't understand
but know are true

if there's nothing needing done
do nothing

don't read
don't watch TV

nothing
but being aware
master of your volatile mind

***

the unexamined life
is not worth living
the over-examined life
is no life at all

***

We need not a new mindset
but freedom from mindsets

at the fountain
of the Tomb of the Unknown Soldier
under Warsaw's
warm autumn morning smile
amidst the colours changing
I am hypnotised
by the sound of the water
rising and falling
and the miraculous rebirth of the city

***

walking with two sticks
the old lady resembles
a cross country skier
she takes a rest on a bench
near where I sit
tilts her head back
to meet the full warmth
of the September sun
arms spread out fully
across the back of the bench
to make the most of the rare autumn heat
dressed like a young girl going for a run
her sunset years are like the early Spring

the wind pulls the dying leaves
from their branches
and they fall giddily randomly
happily to my feet
one lands on my bald area
like a fig leaf to protect my modesty
The rest sit sprinkled on the tarmac
like a mosaic in its early stages

***

sounds flow through my many lives
footsteps of a young woman
in high heels
she's speaking in a foreign language
I don't recognise
water from a nearby burn
comes into earshot
when the shush of the wind dies away
always in the distance
rising and falling
the cars and trucks of busier lives

the sun glints between leaves
in the park
a wee boy moans to his dad
that he's tired
a breeze as subtle as a caress
appears from the stillness
and a branch broken
from last night's storm
lies shadowed on the path

***

the rose does not try to grow
makes no effort to blossom
does not regret its predestined colour

***

the day ends
it had no purpose
no destination
still it fulfilled
gave expression
to the brilliant array
of life forms

do nothing
everything will be done
pull on the handbrake
and you will go on your destined path
what is propelling you
is fear of existing fully

***

the universe is beyond colour and joy
naked in sun and hail
shining without light
dancing without movement
reviving the dead
with pure clear water
in the eternal present

***

everyone is free
but the blinkers are on
we've been told we're in jail
so we're desperately searching
for a door, lock, key
if we stop searching
we can feel the blinkers
and take them off

there's fog on the banking
daylight is pressing through
the trees seem to stretch

stretch even the wind
daylight has dominion
over the scene, fog gone,
the bank unveils
a sea of bluebells.

***

after before [2]
is a void
and a pause
before Next rises
in the pause
no wonders
neither night nor day
a non-sun non-moon
the sleep of dreams that aren't

[2] Based on 'Before' by John Guzlowski

I put out the light
warm and tired in bed
I go to sleep
in my dreams I pray
hold the dying Earth in my arms
saying sorry for our crimes
I heal it with my own tears
life returns
rain soaks my hair
I explore every inch
of the planet's surface
hoping to find my grandmother
when awake
I play in the field of life
but in my dreams it can be dark

walk in the wood and meadows
the whispered breath of shy creatures
my heart beats for nature
that can never die down
this planet contains, it seems
a space where there grows and
blows a force that comes
from before understanding
shimmering in haze and cobwebs
it shakes life everywhere.
my senses - I am in touch with them
like a newborn baby in my arms

(After Fernando Pessoa)

so much junk mail in my mind
unrequested
blocking the doorway
there's a Spring-cleaning required
that will last a lifetime

***

it's cold and fresh
in the distance a dove
sunrise at quarter to eight
a fine day appears
the wind blows the spring leaves
and the y hold fast in their youth

***

to succeed is not necessarily success
to win may be to lose
to be rich can make you poor

when the world tastes of joy
you see the invisible
the shadow of a wren
on a carnation
the ocean in a drop of dew
cascading kindness
on Low Waters Road
the buildings speak
of times gone past
and the pavement
is soft like a cushion

***

silence, already here
in the field alone
birds chatter
catching up
with birdworld news
later, when I'm gone
badgers, squirrels, deer
survey the prospect
of the new dawn

be like the moon
cool, pure, bright

beyond passion
beyond yearning

just being, at peace, in the moment
having nothing, wanting nothing
while all around the delusions whirr on

***

why should I despoil the day
with thoughts of the night?
the night will come when it will
let it come

I choose the day, the light
the sun still shines
when we are on the dark side.

Martin Stepek is author of four books and producer of three documentary films. His first book *For There is Hope*, published in 2012, was an epic poem on the deportation of his father's family to Siberia and the subsequent death of his Polish grandmother by starvation. It won a North American Book Entrepreneur's Award for best bilingual book (English and Polish). It is now also available in English and Spanish.

In 2014 *Mindful Living* was published. It is a series of reflections on how to practise the mental wellbeing techniques of mindfulness in everyday life. *Mindful Living 2* the follow up volume was published on 10 October 2015.

Martin's first film, *The Poetry of Hope,* was produced for the 2013 Edinburgh Fringe Festival as part of an exhibition on Polish-Scottish Heritage. This was followed in 2014 by a film about the extraordinary life of his father, the entrepreneur and philanthropist, Jan Stepek, and in 2015 by the documentary *Mindful Lanarkshire.*

Alongside his creative work, he is a company director, an authority on family-owned businesses, and an experienced mindfulness teacher.

With grateful thanks for the support of

The Scottish Mental Health Arts & Film Festival

SCOTTISH
MENTAL
HEALTH
ARTS & FILM
FESTIVAL

www.flemingpublications.com